Fireflies / Raindrops

M.K. Rion

BookLeaf Publishing

Presentation by *BookLeaf Publishing*

Web: www.bookleafpub.com

E-mail: info@bookleafpub.com

ISBN: 9789357445177

First edition 2021

ACKNOWLEDGEMENT

For everyone who has encouraged me to be able to share my voice with the world.

PREFACE

Content warning: The poetry in this collection deals with heavy themes such as battles with mental health of anxiety and depression, suicide, and abuse.

Spellbound Magic

A puddle!"

I smile at that joyous exclamation as her rain boots race into the wet ground.

Splish, splash.

I see her fascinated by the rippling rings.
She doesn't understand this interaction between
wind, force, and water -
her fingers trace the capillary waves,
the ripples disrupted.

A frown. Step back. A tentative step forward,
the circular rings reform.

A jump off-
the ripples cease,
a return to quietude.
The wide, toothy smile fading,
the infectious giggle dimming.

A frown. A tentative step forward;
she sees the ripples radiate from her rain boot.

I see her smile and laugh - this is a game to her.
Spellbound by water physics.

I smile, laugh.

I wonder now how long it has been since
laughter filled the space around me ?

I Kicked a Pebble Down ...

I kicked a pebble
        down into the gentle stream
        and watched a gentle splash,
        the water spraying up, like a gentle mist.

If only the world
could take a note
of the gentle pebble
and not roar awake
take away everything
and scatter everything.

My grandmother's favorite rocking chair
now broken,
                a roof shingle
now letting the rain pour in,
                my oak bookcase
now splintered,
                the supporting structure
of the house
now gone,
        thrown angrily across the world,

taunting me, leaving me with nothing.

(with anger), I kicked another pebble,
down into the
gentle stream
and watched a
slightly bigger, still gentle splash
the water
spraying up, like a gentle mist.

Not just the world, that destroys everything,
it's the people too
that come in like a raging tornado - and rips
everything apart,

the chair

the roof shingle

the bookcase

the house.

The people - a reminder that
the world is not designed
for people, like me.

I kicked another pebble,
down into the gentle stream,

            and watched a gentle splash,
            the water spraying up, like a gentle mist.

It was so gentle,
almost soft, safe
the misting, never failing.

To this constant earth,
                        that doesn’t give a thought
about who I am.
                        it never mocks or teases, only
the people,
                                                            and I
am the one who let people roar up like a tornado,

but through it all, you (the earth) stayed,
a gentle homogenizing force.

The Storm

Clouds gather overhead
the sun vanishes behind
a low vicious gray.

Rain opens up from the heavens,
a drenching pour.

A clap of thunder,
a bright broken yellow flash through the sky.

The storm;

A nightmare for many,
A fight with the Gods,
feelings of gray, sadness, loneliness,

Despair.

Riverbanks rise with the storm,
white choppy waves crash against the shore,
headlights on, cars screeching,
hydroplaning on asphalt,

destruction.

Drive a little farther,
gray opens up to blue,
rain vanishes behind,
thunder a distant mnemonic sound,
lightning now miles gone,
yellow flashes giving way to a yellow sun.

Brighter days ahead,
harsh memories put behind,
driven away by the storm.

Another Day Waiting

There was a time,
not so long ago
where your news
where your lack of forthcoming
put me in a jail cell
where I was stuck
Waiting.

Waiting on news
if your heart would beat
again,
If your eyes would open
to another day.

Now,

I wait patiently,
stone hearted,
stone faced,
stoic.

I would like to care,

deep down I think I do care,
but the coldness, anger
takes over
replaying all the times
You hurt me so
where I would never be
                                        good enough
                                        perfect enough

For Your undefinable high expectations
For me to be
        the person you never were,
                                                  never would
be.

Now,
forgiveness long past,
I wait patiently,
an emotionless paralyzed cold stone statue
until you lived to breathe
Another day,

and the cycle of
hurt and pain
would continue again.

You Will Never Know

You will never know
how much Hurt,
                    Despair,

Pain that you cause.

Each word,
          a staggering dagger
                    to my heart.

(Breaking the fragile glass into a million pieces).

          A punch to the stomach.

(A crumpled defeated doubled over useless ball
on the ground).

Each text message,
each call,
each conversation,

My breath behind held -

waiting those paralyzing seconds
for the response:

            civil, or destined to crush

each time,
more paralyzing, soul crushing
than the last -

            Anger,

of why I must always be expected
to rise up from broken down
to have that power
always dangling overhead,
            Always -

Out of reach.

Trapment of the Abuser

Giant,
large and looming,
presence everlasting
everywhere my eyes lay
everywhere my feet walk
every location, walls close in
the ceiling crushes down,
air suffocates
as your cruel cruel face
stares just out of reach and
Laughs.

Laughs at the pain
laughs at the life being drained from me,
a bloodless vampire,
Laughs at the hurt, the tears
streaking down my cheeks,
Laughs at my scream
that no one hears.
Laughs as I squeeze my eyes shut
trying to block out the pain, him,

Until he can be nothing more than a tiny black dot, drifting away on the horizon.

Away

Away,
I want you away
all the hurt you caused,
Away.

The power
of you inside my brain
constantly holding

harsh memories
that never escape me.

When I look back,
I never see
A girl, hand in hand
with a father, laughing,
skipping, pigtails bouncing
down the drive.

When I look back,
I always see
one little girl (me) hiding
too afraid of you
not wanting to ever
meet your menacing eyes
that I am, for the first time

afraid to share,

One little girl (me) hides
so you could never
get the change again
to berate the disappointment
You raised.

Takes me years
to admit
I am a victim
takes me years
to raise both hands over my head
and say

“I am a warrior.”

I will always rise
above you
You nothing more
than a fading figure
in my past.

You’re away,
gone,
to where my eyes never have to take in your
sight
again.

Away.

My Shadow

Every time I look back
Your large shadow lurks
never more than a
step back,
black arms reaching
pulling me back,
back under your control,

Forming me into
nothing more than Your shadow
and I'm too tired

            of fighting
            of running away

I no longer fight
and fade away
into Your shadow

That wanted me all this time.

My eyes flash open
pulse rapid, fast

as my eyes dart around
carefully, cautiously,
they making sure
He is not there.

He is not.

A dream,
I am alone,
my own shadow
not his,

Except it's not just
A dream, when every night I
wake up panting, hoping
that He is not a part of

Me.

The part I hate most?

The refusal to fight.
I want to believe
I am stronger than Him,
And His power.

I wonder though,
if the dream were real
what would happen

If He always were
a step behind?

Or if His shadow were a part of me?

That is not a life
I want to live again,
would I be strong enough
to leave Him again?

He almost got me the first time.

Those years, the worst
a fight for out,
a question of
my inner strength
Each, and Every Day.

Too painful to recounter
the words

“I’m sorry”
“I will never be good enough.”

Prominent.

Simple sentences,

No, simple devastating sentences
is all that remains from those years
from the not so distant past
but it is enough,

Enough,
that I always know
You're not a step behind,

You're a part of me.

Perhaps,
that's what makes the dream so terrifying.

I never want to admit
You're still there,

The dream speaks the truth,
one I've spent years avoiding,

Except that I will
never stop fighting
to erase You,

and be My own,
with My own shadow.

Sight of the Fireflies

Through a blurry lens of tears
I see so clearly
all that was denied,
not from others taking,
what I was taking -

an ability to see
the flashing fireflies
the young girl chasing them
fascinated by the creature
reinstating magic
in an oh, so cruel universe.

- What I was taking
from myself
consumed in a dark,
dark tunnel, blacker than a
midnight sky,
where the light shines no longer
where there's no chance of the mystical
magical fireflies,
inside the world of
Blood
Shattering glass

Piercing skin
Pain
Scars
trying to hide how broken
how beaten down
I have been
living through years of
Pain,
Of a heart that will not control its beat,
a beat not so steady anymore
A body where most of its
Blood has spilled
stained on the floor,
the knife, the defender,
the harmer,
Words said worse
than bones snapping,
the face, the abuser,
My everlasting thoughts.

Tears from words, worlds
blurs my vision
yet I see
a beauty taken
that inability to see
flashing fireflies
young and innocent
unharmed me,
the me I see.

Through a blurry lens of tears,
through a shattering glass tunnel,
the me I see.

Anxiety

Pressed against the glass
pale hand
face, haunted
shadowed by the
paralyzing, long shaky breaths
shorter, louder,
each breath a
more desperate cry for

"Help!"

She screams.
Silence.

She turns to the next wall-
faced with only
another reflection of herself.
Her eyes of pain,
moistened by sadness
stare back.

She turns to the next wall -
hoping for a door,
a way out,
faced with only

another reflection of herself.

Her last chance,
she turns again,
again a shadowed reflection.

"Help!"

Her mirror cell doesn't budge
and the only things she sees
                                        a body filled with scars
                                        every flaw

and
                                        her silent haunting
screams
 that
                                        no one besides herself,
                                        can see, can hear.

Each breath gasp
more desperate.
pressure mounts down,
the mirrors close in.

Girl is now huddled,
knees up, pressed against the slow beat of her chest,
arms wrapped around herself,

compression feels good.
She - lets - out - one - more - desperate - cry.

"Help!"

Panic, anxiety
No One sees.
"You'll be fine," they say
failing to understand
the unfolding crisis
until the mirrored walls force her in.

They collapse.
shards of broken glass, replaced by
concrete walls
air replaced with the open ceiling
Girl can breathe again,
She leans against the wall,
the wall supports,
until she is ready to step into the air again.

Others aren't so lucky.

Imperfections

I wish the world would stop staring
of every flaw, every imperfection of beauty,
every scar,
faded or anew.

No one knows the stories
the pain that lays behind every mark
the story beneath every scar of
sadness, of pain.

Constant comparison to others
what the others perceive
have shown the ugliness of them
that we know all to well in this world,

The imperfections stare back
in each mirrored reflection
every morning, every night,
without the eyes of others watching,
our eyes watch our own.

Each imperfection is already known,
the shame already had,

And when its finally beaten

the reflection holds
a little less hatred,

And I venture outside
to try not let society beat me down,
I see the eyes
judging my flawed skin
the scars of my anxiety
that in a normal person wouldn't be there,
my vampire pale skin shows every crude mark,
my unproportional giraffe like limbs.

I am not them,
But I am Me,
doesn't matter what they see,
what I see,
as my body is not a temple,
and instead bares of the war of this world.

The Song of Your Scream

Scream
like you never have before,
Scream,
like no one is listening to the hollowing
emptiness of your soul

… because they are not.

Scream,
and let it out,
all the emotions,
that have been taught
for us to conceal,

and Scream
and let your howl
be carried among the wind
a bird now carrying
your not so gentle tune.

Scream,
like you're the only left,

and all alone,

… because you are,

As who is listening?

As in all truth,
we are all alone
in a world of so many
No One hears

and we stand alone
on the mountaintops
and Scream
letting the truth
truth of horrors out
let it out,
let it be carried through the dark woods.

A not so gentle song,
one all the same,

the scream that lets you out
carries you through the world
even if it's only nature
lifting your song.

I See You Hiding

I see you hiding
I see your brown eyes, one full of spark -
Empty
Your pale face, now almost like a ghost,
Almost.

I still see you behind all the faces,
front row, now back
too scared to raise
a shaking hand
against the world,
that hurt you so.

Too scared to make a sound,
can not now even muster a whisper
against the chatter
never ending chatter
of the outside world
that hurt you so.

Your bright smile,
always a light
known to illuminate someone's day -
Gone,
lips pressed together

too scared to reveal that smile
to the world
that hurt you so.

The world that you left you broken
too broken
to reveal your beauty
to all the scary faces
that hurt you so.

I see you hiding,
determination is me
to let you see the world again,
find the beauty within,
to the world see you,
appreciate your own glowing beauty,
your curiosity, intelligence, humor,
your smile.

I see you,
I'll share your burden,
I'll lift you back up again,
help you fly again
and not let the world break you so
if you'll let me.

Don't Give Up, Just Yet

How do I tell her
it's only going to get harder
that everyday will become
a thicker trudge through the mud,
that there will be times
life may not be worth living,
but to keep going, keep living
when each day it's harder
to open the sad eyes
lift up the heavy head
from paralyzing chains
to keep smiling
despite all the pain
to never let go of the ledge
despite how bad everything gets?

How do I tell her
to not give up,
not just yet?

That the battle everyday living
will make you stronger, more fearless

that there will be
                    walls to lean into
                    shoulders to cry into
                    smiles to be shared
                    battles to be won
                                        or lost joys
                                        or frustrations
                    and anxious excitement?

Do I tell her that? The horrors of life,
only things seen right now
could give away
to burdened happiness?

How do I tell her,
(the younger me),
to not give up, not just yet
when the road ahead
is a treacherous ride,
when the happiness can’t yet be seen,
even though there may be a rainbow at the end
of the yellow road?

The Struggle to Choose to Live

Dirt crumbles beneath,
and she slides back down
grunting, sighing
          a hand reaches back up,
grasping for anything she can find

a root.
Sturdy enough
to hold her feet?
so she can reach the ledge
and peek above the ground

          to where the sun is starting to shine.

out of the tunnel,
a suffocating coffin
where days filled up
gasping, grasping
for the slightest bit of air

When there was none.

Until she grows tired
and faced with two choices;

To live, or to die,

and she chose to live.

Chose to
            climb up
reach the glowing
orb, out of the stormy sky,
catch it, grab it,

Reclaim that power (once taken away).

That power that shoved her
in the suffocation coffin,
leaving her
gasping, grasping
for the slightest bit of air.
She reaches the ledge
(barely, her footing lost underneath her)
      reaches up, reaches forward,

and grabs the glowing orb,
smiles in its warming light,
and throws it back up,
clearing the stormy skies.

and she chose to live.

The Other End

In the darkness
I see the light
within the trapment of drenching rain
the story of tears
from crying that never steps
from the pain and hurt
betrayal of my own self
the nightmare of my mind,
I see the end, the other side,
the sun peeking behind the rain
the smile erasing the pain.

One Old, One Young

Hands clasped,
one old wrinkled, one young
a bright yellow umbrella
shielding them from
cold rain,
stepping forward.

My youthful body
on top her old one,
I worry she may break under my weight -
she insisted,
her smile grows
her fingers follow old pictures
that tell her life story
her growing family tree.

Hands clasped,
one old wrinkled frail, one young,

colorful streamers line
balloons bounce to ceilings
tiny flames dance upon candles

upon a birthday cake
celebrating our two days of birth,
one and the same.

Hands clasped,
one old wrinkled frail breaking, one young,

our smiles freeze in place,
cameras snap,
a frozen photograph,
frozen moments in time

lining dying walls -

memories from time long past,

snippets from fading memories,
where there will be
nothing left

as the dying walls die
and the photographs,
the memories
come crashing down
shatters into a million pieces
around the one young girl, me,
once joyous, now dying,
the last line to the pictures
before everything is gone.

Hands clasped,
two old but young
under a bright yellow umbrella
walking out of the rain
to the Sun.

Strength of the Storm

Crystal choppy waves
a quiet, yet thunderous roar
crashes against toes
dipped in the white slippery sand,

crashes against ankles,
coated in the same,
as the gray menacing clouds roll in
juxtapositioning against the pearl blue of above,
the powerful yellow light
fading beneath the nearby storm.

Waves crash,
above the ankles,
splashing against the shins
the winds pick up
shakes the hair out
a slap against the face,

a sign what's coming
more powerful than the strength built
more evil than good forces to overcome

yet, despite their strength,
this storm is too much,
the water too overwhelming.

toes tighten against, curl into
the sinking sand,
marking the place (of disappearance)

(Or appearance),

as one emerges from the wave that crashed
overhead, soaked, water dripping,
but still standing as the storm passes on.

It was stronger than her,
more overwhelming than what she know, but
still she stood
refusing to be beaten down
knowing the sun will once more shine against
the pearl blue reflecting against
clear calm pools of sand.

Landing/ Falling

Always one hand away
I'm so close
yet slipping off the ledge.

A single grasp,
a single step
a way from reaching the destination
to which I will never land,

or at least
it is what it feels
always out of a reach,
never landing,
spiraling towards the ground
nothing more than a heaping lump
of Failure,

(when it doesn't have to be),

a mind so evil
defeats the effort forward
turns every try
into nothing more
than a fall

barreling me far
so far down
to where the top
Impossible to reach
again,

... (or is it)?

Is it
that impossible to reach
to land
to stick the landing

or is it all
that needs to happen is to
to conquer the demon
that lives inside us all

and is that
the real success of us all?
not worth the time
the barreling falls
only with the try
that conquers
our devastating little voice
that is always a negative fall
away from their top…

… but isn’t our top

our goal, desires,
What we make it?
and not the work of the devil
living inside.

They can fall,
Not I.

My Colorful Story

Words
black and white
printed on each page
that tells my story

of Years of being broken,

Years of my differences,
speech, movement,
always a target on my back,

to Years of constant worry to be outside the
protective walls of home
where I would be broken down
into a puddle of nothing
more than fears
and wet tears

Years of abuse,
betrayal of my own flesh and blood,

questioning me, myself

Years of prisons
of my within my own walls

trapped within physical walls

Years of my mind betraying me
making every day
a battle hard to be fought
each month, a war
my own breath,
now nothing more than a dream,

a wish to be desired.

Now these words,
stirring up of hard lives past,
days wasted,
of bullies winning,
months living.

A story printed,
a story of failures, pains, and triumphs,
My story.

My story,
unlike the black and white words printed,
not just light, joy, or pain,

My story,
colors of an adventure.

Dancing Among the Sunflowers

Ever since I was little,
sunflowers were always my favorite.

I would race out every summer,
watch as the green stems gave way to a beautiful
bloom of yellow petals,
matching the sun beaming down.

I would dance among them,
smiling, laughing.

I never knew why.

I think now,
they radiated that symbol of happiness
that I longed to be.

They represented what I should have had -
I was the green sunflower stem then
too afraid to bloom.

dancing among the yellow petals was all a
dream,
dreaming of what I wanted to be.

Out, loud, proud, happy.

But I’m not dreaming anymore.

I am out dancing among the yellow petals
with the sun beaming down.

Out, loud, proud, happy.

www.ingramcontent.com/pod-product-compliance
Lightning Source LLC
Chambersburg PA
CBHW051738130826
49812CB00033B/905
* 9 7 8 9 3 5 7 4 4 5 1 7 7 *